COWBOYS
of the
AMERICAN WEST

COWBOYS
of the
AMERICAN WEST

PRINCIPAL PHOTOGRAPHY BY DUDLEY WITNEY
TEXT BY B. BYRON PRICE

THUNDER BAY
P·R·E·S·S

Library of Congress Cataloging-in-Publication Data

Price, B. Byron
    Cowboys of the American West / principal photography by Dudley Witney ; text by B. Byron Price.
        p.   cm.
    ISBN 1-57145-032-7
    1. Cowboys – West (U.S.) – Pictorial works. 2. West (U.S.) – History – Pictorial works. I. Title.

F596.P74   1996
978'.0088636—dc20   96-23380
                                                    CIP

Printed in Singapore

 96 97 98 99 6 5 4 3 2 1

Photographs are by Dudley Witney unless otherwise indicated by the credits below.

The Amon Carter Museum, Fort Worth, Texas = *ACM*
The Arizona Historical Foundation = *AHF*
The Erwin E. Smith Collection of the Library of Congress on deposit at
    The Amon Carter Museum = *EES*
The Institute of Texan Cultures, San Antonio, Texas = *ITC*
The Montana Historical Society, Helena = *MHS*
The National Cowboy Hall of Fame and Western Heritage Center,
    Oklahoma City = *NCHF*
The Panhandle Plains Historical Museum = *PPHM*

FRONTISPIECE: A cowboy at the JA Ranch in Texas.

OPPOSITE: The famous Gang Ranch is located in the spectacular Cariboo Mountains of British Columbia.

PAGE 6: A spring-loaded bear trap hangs with antique hardware on the porch of the Siggins Ranch, Cody, Wyoming.

PAGE 7: A horse and cowboy take a breather at the Padlock Ranch, Montana.

PAGE 8: Cowboys readying their mounts at the break of day, Evans Camp Ranch, Buford, Colorado.

PAGES 10 AND 11: Driving cattle at Pitchfork Ranch, Wyoming.

For my grandson, Patrick John Witney. May his ride be full of adventure
—D.W.

For Dad, my favorite cowboy
—B.B.P.

CONTENTS

THE
OPEN
RANGE

Grazing range near Stanley, New Mexico

Watching over the herd during an Arizona
roundup. (*AHF*)

THE OPEN RANGE

Born of economic necessity little more than a century ago, the archetypal American cowboy was the product of free grassland and fertile imaginations. During the late nineteenth century, writers, artists and entertainers transformed this exotic, free-spirited wage earner into a powerful national symbol of democracy that has transcended time and place. This homogenized creation—a heroic blend of pastoral tradition, chivalric code and rugged individualism— scarcely resembled the hired men on horseback who gave him life. Nevertheless, many cowboys themselves eventually embraced and embellished the legend, further obscuring the fading trail of history.

Cowboys in the classic mold appeared in the 1850s, when cattle ranching in Texas emerged as a vital commercial enterprise distinct from other agricultural pursuits. In the same way that the sea lured bold rovers from Marblehead and Nantucket, the prospect of an adventurous life on the prairie appealed to young men of the West. Such an existence, a Texas writer observed in 1860, "is not devoid of risk, and affords to the aspiring mind of youth an opportunity of a display of courage and prowess that is not found in any other department of rural life. The young men that follow this 'Cow-Boy' life, notwithstanding its hardships and exposures, generally become attached to it."

The word "cowboy," however, would not come into general use to describe cattle herders for another decade, when it supplanted more familiar, if prosaic, terms like "stock keeper" and "stock hunter." Yet the trim new label fit, and perfectly described the age, occupation and

Cowboys from the JA Ranch and their horses reflected in a pond, Texas, circa 1900. (*PPHM*)

youthful outlook of most of the horseback herders to whom it was applied. "There were no old men among them," a Colorado newspaper reporter marveled after encountering a typical party of cattle drivers bound for the Republican River in the fall of 1885. "A man of forty was looked upon as a patriarch, one who was entitled to be a candidate for admission to the home of the aged and infirm."

Most cowboys commenced their careers in their late teens or early twenties, although some began much earlier. Notwithstanding the humorous assertion of outspoken Texas cattleman Able H. "Shanghai" Pierce that it was "cheaper to hire cowboys than to raise them," range life came naturally to the rural bred. They were usually at home in the saddle at an early age, and often began roping barnyard pigs and chick-

One of the many African American cowboys of Texas photographed on the Rio Grande Plain. (*ITC*)

ens as soon as they could wield a lariat. Boys as young as six often accompanied their fathers and older brothers on livestock drives or "cow hunts." In 1871, H.P. Cook escorted a herd of longhorns from Texas to Kansas, as a regular hand, at the age of ten. "Back in those days," Cook recalled matter-of-factly more than seventy years later, "lots of boys were good cowboys by the time they were ten years old."

With the rapid expansion of the cattle industry during the two decades following the Civil War, recruits from every region of the United States and many foreign countries swelled the cowboy ranks. No group, however, surpassed in number and prominence those who hailed from Texas. "Cowboys," wrote William A. Baillie-Grohman in the *Fortnightly Review* in 1880,

RIGHT: The cowboys of Matador Ranch taking a break around the chuck wagon. (*PPHM*)

LEFT: A studio portrait of two cowboys in full regalia with lassos and chaps, Victoria, Texas, circa 1890. (*ITC*)

can be divided into two classes: those hailing from the Lone Star State, Texas, the other recruited either from Eastern States, chiefly Missouri, or from the Pacific slopes. . . . The Texans are, as far as true cowboyship goes, unrivaled; the best riders, hardy, and born to the business; the only drawback being their wild reputation. The others are less able but more orderly men.

Runaways and homeless drifters, displaced Civil War veterans and fugitives from justice—all sought sanctuary on the ranching frontier after the Civil War. More than a few of these footloose refugees went by assumed names, and nearly every cowhand eventually acquired a nickname reflecting his place of birth or some distinguishing characteristic, habit or occurrence.

Members of diverse ethnic groups, including sizable numbers of African Americans and Hispanics, also found work on western cattle ranches. Black stock tenders had been fixtures on American plantations since colonial times, and a handful of slaves had risen to positions of responsibility as herders. During the post–Civil War era, blacks comprised the entire labor force on some Texas Gulf Coast ranches. Yet, despite their proven loyalty and prowess as riders and ropers, African Americans often received less pay than white cowboys and were invariably subject to the restrictions and indignities then accorded their race. Celebrated black cowpuncher Matthew "Bones" Hooks, for example, chose the dangerous occupation of horse breaker over other forms of ranch work precisely because there was less competition for the job. "If

ABOVE: Extensive riding tackle and a worn pair of chaps are a cowboy's stock in trade.

LEFT: Cowboys from the Douglas Lake Cattle Company keep watch over their herd in the Nicola Valley of British Columbia.

Several chuck wagons and *remudas* work the open range at the JA Ranch in Texas. (*PPHM*)

it weren't for my damned old black face," Jim Perry of the XIT Ranch lamented of his lack of upward mobility, "I'd have been boss of one of these divisions long ago."

Hispanics, who comprised the largest percentage of professional herdsmen in the Southwest, also suffered from low pay and racial stereotypes that portrayed them as lazy, irresponsible and untrustworthy. Yet cattle barons like Richard King built their fortunes on such men, whose horsemanship, dexterity with a catch rope and ability to manage livestock were matchless.

As cattle rapidly supplanted buffalo on the plains, cowboy life also found appeal with an increasing number of Native Americans. In time, Indian cowboys both tended tribal herds and worked for non-reservation ranches throughout the West. A number of Native bronc riders, like Jackson Sundown, a Nez Percé, and Lakota George Defender, later gained fame in the rodeo arena.

Although many women owned ranches and cattle, few worked openly as regular hands. Some, however, overcame the gender boundaries and social stigmas that discouraged such behavior. Western newspapers occasionally carried intriguing, sometimes sensational reports of females in male attire working as cowhands, drovers and cattle dealers. In 1877, for example, a jilted Nebraska maiden of twenty-two reportedly toiled as a cowboy for several months while tracking down an errant lover. Another woman spent four months in 1888 as a trail-crew drover without being discovered. Three years earlier some forty or fifty "cattle girls" were rumored to be riding the range near San Antonio, Texas. One report claimed that Buffalo Bill Cody tried

The Matador Ranch camp and *remuda*. (*PPHM*)

unsuccessfully to recruit these women, described as "the finest riders in the West," for his Wild West show.

Regardless of their age, race, background or sex, for most the cowboy life was a transitory rite of passage between adolescence and adulthood. Each spring a new crop of greenhorns trekked west to become cowpunchers. The throng always included a host of farm boys called "lints," "cotton tails" and "pumpkin rollers" by range veterans. If they hired them at all, savvy ranch managers usually measured the newcomers' resolve with menial, non-cowboy jobs for a few days before assigning them to a roundup outfit.

There, older hands continued the neophytes' initiation with pranks and jokes that tested both courage and character. Fake Indian attacks and the placing of live snakes and other critters in a greenhorn's bedroll were always good for a laugh. Jokers in one outfit tied one of their number, who pretended to be insane, to a tree. The "madman," of course, broke loose at the appropriate moment and chased a gullible novice out of camp, much to the delight of the rest of the crew. When assigned a string of horses, rookies could expect to draw some of the rankest broncs in the *remuda* to test their mettle.

After passing muster with the old-timers, a novice cowpuncher set about learning his trade. "After the old rawhides had their fun with me as the butt of their jokes," said one appreciative range veteran, "they took me in hand and did all they could to help me learn the work."

The *remuda* and "teepees" of the JA Roundup Camp. (*PPHM*)

A couple of flankers wrestle a roped calf to the ground at an Arizona roundup. The calf will be branded while the flankers hold their catch immobile. (*AHF*)

Inexperienced hands often began their training as horse wranglers or assistants to the chuck-wagon cook. Although many aspiring cowboys, especially those reared in the country, rode reasonably well and were even skilled with a lariat, seasoned buckaroos with a superior knowledge of cattle and horses were years in the making.

Except for periodic fluctuations in the national economy and modest regional variations, the prevailing wage scale for cowboy work remained relatively constant during the three decades following the Civil War. Greenhorns on large outfits usually drew $25 per month, the worthiest top hands $10 to $15 more. The pay scale for ordinary cowboys on the Great Plains in 1885 ranged from a low of $25 per month in Indian Territory, to $30 in the Texas Panhandle, to a high of $40 in Colorado and Montana. Better wages on the northern plains reflected the effects of a weather-shortened working season and the higher cost of living in remote regions. Besides wages, most ranchers provided room and board for their employees, but expected their cowhands to furnish their own saddles and bedrolls.

Despite low pay, long hours, difficult working conditions and expanding demand for labor between 1865 and 1885, cowboys were rarely in short supply. One New Mexico cowman advised another that he could hire plenty of hands if he would "just soak a stake rope in molasses and tie it behind [his] mess wagon and drive through town dragging it."

No one has accurately estimated the number of cowhands actually employed in cattle ranching during its economic peak in the 1870s and 1880s. One reliable source, however, estimated the number of cattle drovers who trailed six to ten million head of cattle and a million horses from Texas to northern markets between the end of the Civil War and the turn of the century at between 25,000 and 35,000 men. According to the *Texas Live Stock Journal*, drives conducted during a single six-month period in 1882 involved approximately 1,400 men, 10,000 horses and 200 chuck wagons.

Professional trail outfits, typically consisting of eleven or twelve men, including the boss; eight drovers; a horse wrangler; a cook; a chuck wagon; and sixty horses, handled some 85 to 90 percent of all trail traffic. Most ranchers found it cheaper and more convenient to engage a contractor to deliver their herd for a set fee than to assign the duty to their regular cowhands.

In contrast to cattle drovers, who made their living taking one herd after another to market, ranch hands spent most of their waking hours systematically gathering, sorting and marking the vast herds of cattle from many outfits that intermingled on the open range. The communal nature of most cow work belied the popular image of cowpunchers as self-reliant loners. By the 1880s regional organizations of stock raisers had divided the range into districts and were conducting cooperative annual gatherings.

A herd of cattle struggle up the banks of the Yellowstone River after being coaxed by cattle drovers across the body of water. Photographed by Evelyn J. Cameron, 1904. (*MHS*)

Depending upon the size of their herds, large ranches fielded one or more roundup crews. At the height of its tenure on the open range, for example, the Block Ranch in New Mexico utilized 4 chuck wagons, 40 to 50 men, and a *remuda* of 500 horses, representing 8 to 10 horses per man. Smaller outfits sometimes combined their resources to equip and operate to a single "pool" wagon.

A typical wagon boss directed the work of from ten to fifteen riders, a cook and a horse wrangler. One or more representatives of distant outfits served on local ranch crews. Each of these "outside" or "stray" men, as they were sometimes known, carried his own string of saddle horses and looked out for the interests of his employer. The more than 300 cowboys who gathered at Tascosa, Texas, for the spring roundup in 1885, for example, included "reps" from Colorado, Kansas, New Mexico and Indian Territory. A hand who worked for the Waggoner Ranch during the 1880s claimed that it was not unusual to see twenty-five to thirty chuck wagons and crews at a single roundup.

Such camps might extend for four or five miles, making it sometimes difficult for men to locate their outfits.

Thirty days prior to the start of work, cowpunchers began to assemble at headquarters, wranglers gathered and shod the *remuda*, and the chuck wagon was outfitted. Most roundups got under way at predetermined times under the direction of a general superintendent or roundup captain familiar with the terrain and possessing the confidence of the participating parties. In some cases, when several outfits worked together, overall command of the roundup devolved on the wagon boss whose home range was being gathered at the time. Regardless of the overall roundup organization, each outfit maintained a separate camp, *remuda* and wagon.

A typical open-range roundup of the late nineteenth century might cover an area of 100 square miles and require several weeks, or even months, to complete, depending upon the weather and the difficulty of the terrain and vegetation. Broken and brush-infested range, which restricted visibility and took its toll on horseflesh, presented special challenges to roundup crews. So did an especially prolonged winter drift of livestock, which forced ranchers to expand the scope of the gathering. When severe Northers depopulated northwestern Texas of cattle during the winter of 1883–84, for example, ranchers in the region abandoned their traditional small-scale regional gatherings in favor of a single huge sweep of the dry reaches of the Pecos River, some 300 to 400 miles to the south. Working seven days a week from sunup to sundown, the busy cowboys gathered as many as 8,000 survivors a day. By the time the last head was collected several weeks later, cattle were strung out on the trail homeward in a continuous body stretching for 40 miles.

By the 1870s, Texas ranchers had begun establishing finishing ranges for their cattle on the northern Great Plains and had exported their cowboys and working methods to the region. Buckaroo outfits from Oregon and California, whose gear, terminology and range practices differed from those of the Texans, were not far behind. Although at least some cultural borrowing was inevitable, each group clung tightly to its own traditions. The sons of the Lone Star State, for example, favored heavy, double-rigged stock saddles and short lariats of rawhide and hemp tied hard and fast to the saddle horn. The

Mess and water wagons roll across the semi-arid plains of the Bell Ranch in New Mexico. (*NCHF*)

Californians, by contrast, depended upon lighter, single-cinch saddles, and wound or "dallied" the free end of their long *reatas* around the saddle horn after catching their quarry.

Although Pacific Coast buckaroos were perhaps a bit more flamboyant than Texans in their dress and the artistic embellishment of their gear, utility took precedence over fashion. Author Hamlin Garland encountered a group of "iron-sided" Colorado cowboys who wore "rough, business overalls and colored shirts—quite generally gray, with dirt and sweat. Their boots were short and very high heeled, and their wide hats and 'slickers' were the only uniform articles of dress."

Short summers and vicious winters, the norm on northern-plains ranges, required modifications in clothing and equipment that included fur coats, caps, gloves and leggings. And whereas southern-based crews, sometimes known as "pot rack" outfits, slept and cooked outdoors throughout the roundup season, those in northern climes were furnished with a mess and bed tents and portable stoves for cooking and heating. When the amount of extra gear outgrew the capacity of the chuck wagon, a second conveyance, known as the "bed wagon," was pressed into service.

As the roundup progressed, diligent chuck-wagon cooks prepared meals in all kinds of adverse weather for ravenous cowhands, who con-

Wagon cook Sam Whitaker maneuvering his heavy cast-iron cookware around the open fire pit on the LS Ranch, 1908. (Photographed by Erwin E. Smith—negative LC S59-68 *EES*)

sumed them without ceremony. "Eating was no delicate business with these centaurs," one writer observed. "It had the certainty and savagery of a farm threshing crew. There were no tables and no frills like cups or butter knives. Some ate standing, others sat on rolls of bedding. Every man helped himself."

Prompt cooks generally served breakfast before daylight, dinner in the early afternoon and supper just before dark. In between, the harried chefs and their assistants, known in some quarters as "hoodlums," almost always moved their camp at least once, and often twice, a day. The typical chuck-wagon fare included beef, salt pork, beans, rice, dried fruit, sourdough biscuits and coffee. A few stingy outfits considered sweets a luxury and carried neither sugar nor molasses. By the early 1880s, however, canned goods were widespread in the cattle kingdom. Cowboys especially coveted the juice of canned tomatoes, which helped counteract the deleterious effects of the gypsum-laden water they were often forced to drink.

Texas outfits were notoriously parsimonious when it came to grub, spending as little as a few cents per day on their hands' subsistence. Their northern counterparts appear to have been fed more liberally. "Live!" chirped a Kansas newspaper correspondent, no doubt exaggerating conditions in Montana. "Why, these cowboys live higher than anybody.

Cowboys look on as their colleagues skin a beef. (*PPHM*)

They have every thing to eat that money can buy, and a cook with a paper cap on to prepare it. The cook is so neat and polite that you could eat him if you were right hungry." All things being equal, miserly management and culinary ineptitude led many seasoned hands to select their outfits based on the quality of the cooking.

Buckaroos gathered and worked the largest cow herds during the spring, when a single large ranch might brand 25,000 or more calves. Like the roundup itself, an efficient branding operation was a model of teamwork. To expedite matters, top hands did most of the cutting and roping. Rarely missing a loop, these lariat men dragged a calf to the branding fire by the head or heels with methodical precision, calling out its mother's brand to insure that the cowboys handling the irons

The Bell Ranch wagon cook shows off the simple yet hearty fare that the ranch hands can look forward to after an exhausting day of working the range. (*NCHF*)

chose the correct mark. Meanwhile, a pair of flankers working on foot met the roper and wrestled his unwilling catch to the ground. After removing the rope they held the animal immobile while other members of the crew applied the brand and ear marks, castrated the male calves, and dehorned and doctored as necessary. On the most efficient crews, the whole process took less than forty-five seconds. Branding 500 head a day was commonplace.

Although cowboys went quietly about their business around cattle herds, they were more animated in camp, engaging in lively campfire conversation that revolved around legendary horses, ropers and riders. Said an eyewitness to one lusty bonfire session, they "sang and boasted and told stiff yarns and exploded in obscenity till time to turn in."

Meal time near Carlsbad, New Mexico, 1888. (*PPHM*)

A rope corral of the Rita Blanca Division of the XIT Ranch, 1898. (*PPHM*)

"None of these men used the slow drawl in their talk," Carl Benedict reminisced. "Most of them could talk very good grammar-school language, and most of them were lively and quick-witted." Profanity peppered the speech of the majority, prompting the Bell Ranch manager to admit that he and his outfit were "a pretty coarse-mouthed bunch generally speaking, if the truth be known." Although few cowboys were overtly religious, cowhand J.W. Standifer remembered a rosy-cheeked farm boy who knelt in prayer at bedtime at the

XIT wagon. "And not a man made a sound; in his simple faith he was their superior."

Many cowboys were keen observers and consummate storytellers. The notably imaginative and verbose among them gained reputations as "augurs," who often matched tales with champion yarn-spinners from other outfits. Other buckaroos possessed a gift for poetry or song, while still others played musical instruments, principally fiddles and guitars.

Some cowboys were illiterate, or nearly so; at least a few, well educated. Reading material was usually scarce in cow camps and, except for the Bible and works by Shakespeare, mostly of the dime-novel, *Police Gazette*, and trade-catalog variety. The learned and unlettered alike held Shakespeare in especially high esteem. "He's the only poet I ever seen what was fed on raw meat," one hand declared. On trips to Chicago with cattle shipments, Montana ranch hand Cabe Adams took in the legitimate theater, while his associates flocked to the red-light district.

Until the 1880s, cowboys in many regions still carried sidearms, knives and rifles, with which they killed predators or wild game, fought outlaws and Indians, and settled personal differences. In 1882 the *Texas Live Stock Journal* encouraged ranchers not to make proficiency with firearms a qualification for employment, saying that "honesty, industry, and experience should be the test of a man's fitness for a cowboy's duties." By this time at least some prudent ranch managers had already banned drinking and gambling and the carrying of sidearms in camp. Most also supported the passage of state and community "pistol laws." Anti-gun legislation notwithstanding, many cowboys continued to stow pistols in their bedrolls or conceal them in chap pockets or shoulder holsters, hidden under coats.

Despite constant pranks, horseplay and banter, cow camps were usually peaceful. But sometimes, personal squabbles could turn violent. And while the aggrieved parties usually settled such matters quickly with fists, occasionally guns and knives came into play. Cowboy John J. Baker recalled one fatal scuffle between a knife-wielding cook and a pistol-packing hand who had repeatedly raided the chuck box for food without permission. Both men died in the affray.

Awake by 4:00 A.M., cowboys turned in early as a rule, by 8:00 P.M.

Roping mounts out of a *remuda*, Texas. (*NCHF*)

in most cases. Until corrals could be erected at strategic points on the range, roundup outfits, working in shifts, kept watch on their herds around the clock. This meant that each member of the crew, except the cook and horse wrangler, worked a full day, then stood guard over the herd for two or three hours every night.

The crew was divided into three to five guards, depending upon the size of the outfit. Relief men got their bearings from the wagon tongue, invariably pointed toward the North Star, and perhaps a lantern hung inside the sheet of the chuck wagon or atop the chuck box as a beacon to camp.

Not many hands carried pocket watches, so most night herders learned to measure the length of their shifts by the movement of the stars or merely guessed at the passage of time. "Sometimes we had watches," one top hand recalled, "but sometimes we stood [guard] by 'heart,' but some of the hands didn't have any heart. When we didn't have watches to tell the correct time, we had lots of jowering [complaining]."

Two men could usually hold 3,000 head without trouble under favorable conditions. Their mounts at a slow walk, the guards circled the herd in opposite directions, often singing or humming softly to calm their wards. Their melodies were so prevalent that night herding was often called "singing to 'em."

During periods of threatening weather, wagon bosses bolstered the guard. "Night riding during a spell of hard weather," cowboy John

Baker remembered, "was no pink tea party." A simple act like striking a match, or even spitting, could start a herd to run. A frightened covey of quail and a crowing rooster ignited at least two stampedes.

At the first sign of trouble, every rider in camp scrambled for his night horse, the most sure-footed in his string, and departed at a gallop for the head of the herd. On attaining the point the horsemen attempted to turn the leaders and mill the herd until it settled down. When the riders could not turn a drove, they simply tried to keep the herd bunched to minimize the number of strays they would have to gather at first light.

The cowpunchers who endured the exhilaration and terror of a stampede never forgot the experience. A few unfortunates did not live through them. Stampedes were, however, not the only dangers facing cowboys in their daily routines. Aggressive bulls, and mother cows defending their offspring, also cost men and horses their lives. Falling mounts and other job-related accidents produced broken bones and career-ending injuries with startling regularity.

That many ranches kept sick or hurt cowboys on the payroll until they had mended was small consolation. Professional medical care was rarely available in the remote areas of ranch country. Cooks generally doubled as doctors, relying upon a variety of home remedies, patent medicines and whisky to relieve a sick or injured hand's pain and suffering.

Cowboy work was seasonal, lasting perhaps six or seven months on the southern plains but only three or four months farther north, where summer was often abbreviated. Upon concluding the fall roundup and delivering the marketable steers to shipping pens or trail crews, ranchers turned out their *remudas* and laid off most of their help. After months of isolation on the range, most of the crew headed for the nearest town, like sailors home from a long voyage, bent on a bath, a new outfit and a good time.

Frontier communities like Dodge City, Kansas; Ogallala, Nebraska; Cheyenne, Wyoming; Miles City, Montana; and Fort Worth, Texas, welcomed the cowboy trade with a variety of outfitters, restaurants, saloons, gambling dens, and houses of prostitution that some called "sally joints." Fabled drinking establishments, with names like the Long Branch, White Elephant, Occidental, and Last Chance, commanded liberal patronage as a cowboy often spent his entire season's wages on

Drying dishes beside the JA Ranch chuck wagon in Texas. (*PPHM*)

a single spree. Some simply left their poke with friendly bartenders, asking only to be notified when it had run out.

The Waco Tap in Fort Worth was typical of the well-appointed establishments prevalent in larger communities. While couples on the lower level shuffled to the square-dancer call, roulette wheels whirled, dice rolled and slick gamblers dealt crooked games of poker and monte. Upstairs, prostitutes entertained customers in their cribs.

While in town, cowboys attempted to live up to their wild reputations. Before local pistol laws took effect, cowboys typically arrived at their destination with a flourish, often discharging their six-shooters until their ammunition was exhausted. Some of the bolder cavaliers even rode their horses directly into saloons, where they demanded service while still in the saddle. Once re-outfitted, many sat for the photographer in poses they thought evocative of their free life.

During shipping season, scores of boisterous, armed and often inebriated cowboys roamed cowtown streets, making crowd control difficult. "These men lived a rough life and enjoyed rough amusement," said one cowtown gun merchant. "The cowboy was not interested in pink teas, ping-pong or any other entertainment of that nature. He desired he-man stuff."

Where alcohol, firearms and women were involved, some violence was inevitable, although rarely to the extent portrayed by the media.

Branding a calf on the JA Ranch. (*PPHM*)

"If one desired a little or a large amount of trouble, he could easily find it," a former ranch foreman recalled, adding, however, that peaceable men were rarely molested.

Most cowboys imbibed at least some alcohol. Eighteen percent of a sample of fifty old-time cowhands interviewed in 1951 characterized their alcohol consumption as excessive. Another 38 percent admitted to moderate drinking. Not quite half the group drank sparingly or not at all. The excessive use of alcohol, in turn, often led to violence, even among friends. "The first glass caused one to see things," recalled frontier saloon keeper William Blevins, "and the next to hear things, and with the third glass every person that talked to you would insult you."

Besides engaging in drinking bouts while in town, some cowboys enjoyed competing among themselves in feats of marksmanship, roping, trick riding and bronc busting. In one of the earliest such competitions, held at Deer Trail, Colorado, on July 4, 1869, several area bronc riders vied for top honors and a new suit of clothes. A Mill Iron Ranch cowboy, who rode a Hashknife outlaw called "Montana Blizzard" to a standstill in fifteen minutes, claimed first prize and was christened "Champion Bronco Buster of the Plains." Such contests became more widespread and formal with time, originating the sport of rodeo.

Ranchers usually retained a handful of cowboys on the payroll over the winter to keep watch for rustlers and distressed stock. Most

A night herder turns in for a few hours sleep at Three Block Ranch, New Mexico, circa 1905. (Photographed by Erwin E. Smith—negative LC 56-188. *ACM*)

of the holdovers occupied far-flung, sparsely furnished dwellings known as "line camps." A pair of hands usually staffed each of these tiny dugouts or cabins, taking turns at cooking and other chores, and patroling their assigned section of the ranch daily. Except for pet cats, employed to keep mice at bay, and an occasional freighter, who delivered mail and provisions, camp men led a mostly lonely and monotonous existence.

During the early spring, however, the pace quickened as camp men kept busy rescuing cattle bogged in creek beds and water holes. Many winter-weakened bovines, hounded by heel flies, became stranded and had to be extracted from their predicament by means of strong ropes, stout arms and short-handled shovels. Although bog riders took care to avoid breaking an animal's legs or horns, or choking it to death with their ropes, accidents were inevitable. One range authority estimated that fully 80 percent of the liberated stock never recovered from the ordeal.

Besides watching for bogged animals, camp men also had to be alert to prairie fires. At the first sign of trouble, the entire ranch rode to the scene of the blaze. There they fought the flames by hand, using brooms, wet gunny sacks and saddle blankets, and sheet-iron and chain drags pulled between two horsemen. Sometimes the firefighters killed cattle and dragged their bleeding carcasses across the fire line. Only a few larger

Startled cattle resist the roundup. (*AHF*)

ranches took the extra precaution of plowing firebreaks.

Unemployed cowboys, meanwhile, sought odd jobs in nearby communities or returned to their home towns or families to await the beginning of the spring gathering the following April. A few energetic types spent the winter harvesting predators and collecting the cash bounties that some ranches and county governments offered for wolves, coyotes and prairie dogs. Other out-of-work hands turned predators themselves, prowling remote ranges, looking to steal heavy, unbranded calves overlooked in the summer and fall roundups. More artistic and ambitious thieves changed existing brands with the help of a "running iron." If deftly done, a bogus brand was hard to detect until the animal's hide was removed.

Some ranchers tried to foil cow thieves by close-herding their

VVN Ranch preparing to ship four hundred head of cattle from Texas to Colorado, 1903. (*NCHF*)

animals during the winter and establishing salt licks near water holes and winter camps to help keep the animals from wandering. In the fight against rustling, they not only depended upon loyal employees, but also hired stock detectives to work roundups along with regular hands, and brand inspectors who seized stolen stock at shipping points and river crossings. Cattle raisers also organized regional protective associations, which, in the absence of formal legal institutions, sometimes dispensed vigilante justice. Western juries, however, were notoriously lenient in rustling cases, and relatively few cow thieves were successfully prosecuted.

As ranching became more profitable, cattle more valuable, and corporate investment more common, cattlemen began to abandon the wasteful practices that had long characterized the business. They discouraged the reckless handling of livestock and adopted strict rules governing their care and maintenance. Said an observer of one manifestation of the new attitude, "These men do not allow their hands to dash those horses around just for the fun of the thing." Demanding bosses also began firing hands who employed ill-fitting saddles and severe bits and spurs. Management's tough new attitude did not, however, stop one indifferent hand from killing a company mule that had resisted a bridle. "This Syndicate outfit has got two million dollars to buy mules that a fellow can bridle," he told a friend before stalking off to inform the boss that the mule had died from eating too much corn.

Before the advent of large-scale corporate cattle companies during the 1870s and 1880s, many cowhands accepted at least part of their wages in cattle or invested their meager earnings in livestock. Others managed herds on shares in exchange for a portion of the increase, typically 25 percent, depending upon whether or not the herdsman pro-

A cattle train waits for the boarding of its freight. (*NCHF*)

vided his own horses, gear and keep. This system relieved ranchers of labor costs and insulated them somewhat from theft because losses were typically deducted from the herder's share.

As competition for the range intensified, however, small-scale operators were increasingly at a disadvantage, and the opportunity for a cowboy to own his own herd diminished. The new corporate heavyweights usually prohibited their employees from personally owning horses and cattle. Although such rules were widespread, there were notable exceptions. Montana cattle baron Granville Stuart, for example, allowed at least some of his trusted employees to run their stock with his outfit. According to one hand who built a substantial herd with Stuart's help, "Many men who started on this basis were the Cattle Kings of later years." George Littlefield's LFD outfit was another of the exceptions. "They'd let you run all you could get," recalled a Littlefield wagon boss. "There wasn't no limit."

Despite booming conditions and fabulous profits enjoyed by many ranchers during the two decades following the Civil War, cowboys witnessed only modest improvements in their living conditions, and almost none in their wages. Yet by the 1880s, only a few vocal critics of these inequities had emerged. Giving most cattle barons more credit for benevolence than was their due, one Colorado newspaper gently suggested that, because of

the nearness and cheapness of all the material out of which comforts can be secured, we know that every consideration of a moral and pecuniary nature—inducement beneficial to pride and pocket—will lead cattle owners to better provide for both the mind and bodily comforts of their hands. Good, comfortable ranch houses should take the place of tents and dugouts; better beds should be ready for the cowman when he reaches the ranch after a long, hard day's ride in the rain and sleet; generous, wholesome food, properly cooked and served in neat, clean dishes, should be placed before him.

Union organizers made scant headway among the fiercely independent equestrians of the plains, and the few scattered instances of labor unrest among members of the cowboy tribe did little to improve their lot. The most celebrated job action occurred in 1883, when cowboys struck five ranches in the Texas Panhandle for higher wages, demanding $50 per month for regular hands and cooks and $75 for range bosses. After more than two months of peaceful inactivity, however, the strikers disbanded without achieving their goals. Some returned to cowboy jobs in the face of blacklisting. Others moved into New Mexico and began rustling from their former employers.

Some cowboys registered their displeasure with management in

BELOW AND RIGHT: The bronc buster's occupation, breaking wild horses to be added to the *remuda*, is among the most dangerous and well-paid jobs of the ranch. (*MHS*)

RIGHT: Cowboys pin unbranded calves to the ground on the northern plains of the XIT Ranch. (*PPHM*)

LEFT: The bookkeeper's office at the JA Ranch in Texas. (*PPHM*)

BELOW LEFT: Cattle being dipped to rid them of ticks on the Matador Ranch. (*PPHM*)

more subtle ways. When, for example, the boss of the Prairie Cattle Company eliminated canned goods from the chuck-wagon menu, irate hands slaughtered a heifer each afternoon in protest, leaving most of the meat for the wolves.

By the mid-1880s the cowpunchers of the open range found themselves part of a rapidly changing order and possessors of a freshly rehabilitated public image. "The cowboy is not now the reckless semi-savage of ten years ago," Texas rancher C.C. Slaughter observed in an 1882 *Chicago Times* interview. Slaughter and his fellow revisionists repeatedly challenged the wild, violent, rude, rough, profane depictions of cowboys prevalent in the press and popular literature, emphasizing instead their more positive character traits as loyal, honest, reliable and intelligent employees. Almost overnight the "perfect desperadoes" of the pulps were transformed, Cinderella-like, into princes of the prairie. Meanwhile, the forces of technology were already conspiring to bring an end to the free grassland that had sustained the cowboy's unbounded lifestyle. Barbed wire, railroads, farmers and females would all continue to shrink the cowboy's domain in the decades to come and forever threaten the pastoral world that gave him life.

THE
NEW
ORDER

The waters of the Rio Grande, lifeline of the southern cattle industry, twist through the desert range near Hatch, New Mexico.

PREVIOUS PAGE: A rancher builds a dam to divert spring water into a hayfield near Snowmass, Pitkin County, Colorado.

The Goose Lake Cattle Company ranch slopes
to the banks of the Bow River in southern
Alberta.

ABOVE: The Padlock Ranch lays claim to this precious water hole nestled in the Wolf Mountains along the Montana–Wyoming border.

LEFT: The rugged range of the Shoshone Mountains looms over northwest Wyoming.

FAR LEFT: A dug-out spring creates an oasis for cattle at the Perry Minor Ranch near Bindloss, Alberta.

At San Julian Rancho near Point Conception, California, it has been necessary to diversify beyond cattle raising to the less glamorous, but more profitable, enterprise of mining for diatomaceous earth.

Despite its forays into more profitable mining ventures, the old Mexican land grant of San Julian Rancho still grazes some of the most lush fields found in the American Southwest. Unlike most of the great old ranchos of the nineteenth century, San Julian Rancho has been able to survive the engulfing urban-sprawl of California, precisely because of its ability to remain competitive through diversi-fication beyond cattle ranching.

The once Spanish rancho land of the Santa Yncz
Valley has been subdivided into small ranches
and horse farms that comprise some of the most
valuable real estate in California.

OVERLEAF: Corralled cattle on the JA Ranch,
Clarendon, Texas.

The sprawling plateau south of Choteau, Montana.

A summer range in the Big Horn Mountains, Wyoming.

OVERLEAF: Winter on the New Mexico range lands.

Spring flurries near Durango, Colorado.

A surprised cow takes shelter from the winter's
first snow on a high plains ranch in Colorado.

A thin layer of snow blankets the ranches south of Buffalo, Wyoming.

OVERLEAF: A chilly early morning on the James Ranch near Durango, Colorado.

A summer storm
approaches near
Ridgeway, Colorado.

Although mostly given over to development and agriculture, the land grant rancho Mission Viejo in Orange County, California, still leaves some unplowed land for ranching.

Grazing land in the eastern Alberta Neutral Hills
runs adjacent to the flats of the Saskatchewan
wheat fields.

A dust storm darkens the sky over the Texas Panhandle.

An early evening full moon gazes down on New Mexican fields.

Needing less food and water than cattle, sheep
are more suited to grazing on the arid winter
ranges of Wyoming.

Summer on the slopes of the Big Horn
Mountains, Wyoming.

OVERLEAF: Erected by herders as markers and to
relieve boredom, rock cairns add to the desolate
landscape of the Shoshone Mountains.

The lush irrigated grasslands of Douglas Lake,
British Columbia.

A range preservation and research program at
the Research Ranch near Fort Huachuca,
Wyoming.

ABOVE: An Alberta summer.

LEFT: A country road in Alberta.

OVERLEAF: Ranch in spectacular southern
Alberta.

Tranquil early
evening near
Sheridan, Wyoming.

Bales of hay are
found at the end of a
ranch hand's rainbow.

THE
NEW
ORDER

By the early 1880s, the once inexhaustible carpet of free grass on which cowboys plied their now well-publicized trade appeared all too finite. Fueled by vast eastern and foreign investment capital, the long and exceedingly profitable post–Civil War beef boom had also encouraged rampant overcrowding, overgrazing and overproduction. In 1884 cattle prices began to weaken, and stockholder dividends, which the previous year had surpassed 25 percent for some ranching companies, began to tumble. The decline sharpened in 1885 and 1886 as prolonged droughts and vicious blizzards struck ill-prepared Great Plains herds and ranchers with a vengeance. In the Texas Panhandle alone, an estimated 150,000 to 200,000 cattle perished, some cattle raisers losing 90 percent of their herds. Losses were even worse in Montana, Wyoming and the Dakotas. The following spring, cowboys throughout the plains harvested more cowhide with their skinning knives than they branded with hot irons.

Struggling to meet the demands of anxious creditors, hard-pressed ranchers dumped the emaciated survivors of the winter debacle on an already depressed market, with predictable results. By 1887 beef steers brought only 20 to 25 percent of the 1883 selling price on the Chicago market. Stock cattle fared even worse, with cows bringing scarcely $5 a head, down from a peak of $35. Some shipments failed to return even their transportation costs. Others found no buyers at all and were returned to the range unsold. As drought and depression lingered into the 1890s, cattle companies failed by the score, throwing many cowboys out of work. Wages for hands lucky enough to retain a job dropped to as little as $15 per month.

Of even greater long-term import, the ecological disaster of the mid-1880s hastened trends, some already evident, that would soon bring an end to the haphazard open-range style of ranching and the freewheeling cowboy life that accompanied it. In their stead rose a more careful and diversified system, smaller in scale and rooted in Midwestern husbandry practices.

Barbed-wire fences, which would have the greatest technological impact, had appeared on the range a decade earlier, thanks to Illinois farmer Joseph F. Glidden's practical design and patent of 1874. Few ranchers immediately embraced the new invention, however, and many opposed it. Some believed that the inhumane barbs would spread injury and disease among their herds. Wire salesmen had to convince others that their product, which cost between $200 and $400 a mile to install, could withstand the challenges of fickle weather and determined livestock.

The benefits of the new fencing material, particularly on the treeless plains, overcame every objection save that of a small but determined group of "free grassers," who resented any effort to close the public domain to their herds. Many disgruntled members of this group simply moved their herds to less hospitable regions, where the range remained open. The diehards fought the new enclosures with a determined campaign of fence cutting in a futile attempt to delay the inevitable occupation of the land by farmers and smaller stock raisers. "There wasn't a fence post standing anywhere," a rancher's son recalled after a visit from some destructive Wise County, Texas, wire cutters. "When they'd cut the wire between two posts, they'd also lassoed the posts and drug 'em down." A gang of fence maulers destroyed another persistent Texas stock raiser's barbed enclosure not once but twice, severing every wire and sawing every post in half.

The new barriers invited not only wholesale destruction, but also petty vandalism, as impatient cowboys, chafing at the distance between gates, created their own ad hoc openings with impunity. Kindling seekers on the treeless prairies also targeted fence posts. One New Mexico ranch hand admitted removing every other post of a neighbor's fence for ten miles to provide emergency fuel. Ranches with inviting stands of cedar and scrub oak had to exercise vigilance

A rancher could not be expected to raise many cattle on such arid land in New Mexico.

to keep poachers from denuding their range of timber for fence posts.

As the destruction of fences spread, stock raisers' associations employed detectives, offered rewards and lobbied the federal government and state legislatures for tougher laws and prison sentences for perpetrators. In time, aggressive action by the Texas Rangers and other law-enforcement officials reined in the lawlessness. As in rustling cases, however, local juries were reluctant to convict fence cutters on criminal complaints, and only a few served jail time.

The fence cutters directed much of their ire against stockmen guilty of fencing the public domain without authority in an attempt to control critical water and pasture resources. "It is natural, perhaps, for these companies to exercise all the power given them toward perpetuating their existence, against which settlement is a growing menace," declared one cow-country newspaper. Another authority estimated that, by 1887, errant cattlemen had illegally enclosed more than three million acres of government-owned grass. Disagreements over fencing rights would persist in some regions for more than two decades.

By limiting the winter drift and mixing of cattle on the open range, barbed-wire fences enabled cattlemen to trim their labor costs, in some cases by as much as 80 percent. Cross-fencing the range into smaller pastures and constructing pens, corrals and chutes at roundup grounds and other strategic points reduced the number of men needed to gather and hold herds during roundups and brandings and eventually brought an end to night herding as well. An aggressive fencing program in the Texas Panhandle during the summer and fall of 1886, for example, prompted the *Tascosa Pioneer* to remark: "Many are the hands who have been turned off during the past month or six weeks, and who are lying about in idleness or arranging to visit the old folks down the country until work opens up again in April or May. The majority of the ranches will get along through the winter with fewer employees, perhaps, than for some winters previous." Spur Ranch managers credited fencing with reducing the average number of hands employed monthly in all capacities from a high of seventy-two in 1887 to only forty-nine two years later. The number continued to decline as a result of drought and depression until, by 1896, the average reached a low of only twenty-five. By 1894, Murdo Mackenzie, boss of the nearby Matador Ranch, reported needing only eight men to look after nearly a half-million acres between the fall and spring roundups. Wages and room and board for all eight amounted to a modest $320 a month.

In addition to aiding distressed livestock, keeping watch for rustlers and other predators, and turning away unwanted trail herds, these fence riders tried to prevent drifting cattle from crowding and breaking through fences during severe storms. On their daily rounds they always packed a hammer and a pair of pliers, or a specialized fencing tool, and extra fence staples with which to mend broken or detached wire. Special crews and equipment sent from headquarters repaired major breaks and broken posts, and replaced "water gaps" washed out by floods. By the late 1880s a few ranchers were even experimenting with electric fences, although rarely with long-term success.

Despite the obvious benefits, working around barbed wire could be dangerous and, on occasion, even fatal. "Barb wire," said one wary ex-cowpuncher, "is a hard thing to get used to, and is hard to see when you've got your mind on penning stock. In fact, if it wasn't for the posts, you'd never think of wire while working stock." While corral-

The waters of the Animas Creek have been dammed and diverted to make the Ladder Ranch of southern New Mexico a possibility.

ling a bunch of wild mustangs, one New Mexico cowboy died when his mount encountered an inconspicuous barbed-wire fence and threw him, breaking his neck.

The proliferation of the barbed barriers, coupled with an expanded railroad network and tick-fever quarantines, also brought an end to the long drive as a means of conveying cattle to market or to finishing ranges on the northern plains. By the mid-1890s the last large herds were wending their way northward from Texas to Montana. Ten thousand head of two-year-old XIT steers, divided into five herds, each accompanied by six cowboys, a cook and a horse wrangler, made one of the final journeys in the spring of 1895.

Although cowboys continued to deliver cattle to shipping pens, sometimes several hundred miles distant, the specialized occupation of trail driver disappeared by the turn of the century. Regular hands made most of the latter-day drives, invariably trailing smaller herds than before. Their course often meandered in long detours around ranches whose owners discouraged such encroachments. Even the most accommodating ranchers insisted that passing drovers maintain a steady pace. In a few regions, however, cooperative cattlemen established formal lanes over which trail herds might travel unimpeded.

The cross-fencing of pastures also accelerated the introduction of expensive breeding stock and the eventual upgrading of herd quality through the introduction of the Durham, Shorthorn, Hereford and Polled Angus blood. The process of blending the bloodlines of more-domesticated breeds with that of feral longhorns took many generations to achieve. But as ranchers took a more scientific approach to cattle raising, they began to frown on the rough handling of stock, including the use of hide-splitting stock whips and, especially, unnecessary roping.

The prospect of winning prize money, trophies and bragging rights at the roping contests that proliferated throughout the late-nineteenth-century West encouraged many cowboys to hone their skills, often at the expense of their employers' livestock. Ranchers, in turn, pressed for laws prohibiting such competitions under the guise of the prevention of cruelty to animals. "Roping is an occupational disease with [cowboys]," observed one latter-day hand, "and one that cattle owners are forever and vainly trying to cure. . . ."

Although regular ranch work offered cowpunchers plenty of legitimate opportunities to "shake out a loop," the new strictures struck at the heart of cowboy tradition. Skill with a lariat had always epitomized top hands like Wash Tankersley and Charley Binson, who between them once snagged 500 calves at a single branding without missing a loop. Writer Richard Harding Davis called an equally impressive 1898 roping demonstration by *vaqueros* of the King Ranch, "as remarkable a performance in its way as I have ever seen."

Prudent ranchers discouraged not only roping, but also the rushing of cattle on the move. "The best time that a herd of cattle ever made was made in a walk," foreman Harrison Smith of the LX Ranch reminded his crew. "They will save more flesh, and flesh is money, and if the cattle don't make money, our jobs are in question."

An irrigation canal snakes across the plateau near Montrose, Colorado.

The wagon and range bosses who issued such orders were usually themselves experienced top hands, men of "education and ability," according to one informed observer. Most began as lowly horse wranglers and worked up to positions of responsibility over a period of years. In recognition of their talent, "top screws," as cow bosses were sometimes known, usually drew two or three times the pay of regular hands.

Successful wagon bosses combined leadership with a superior knowledge of cattle and horses. While enforcing upper management's rules against drinking, gambling and abusing livestock, the best foremen treated their hands with equity and respect. Longtime cowboy J.C. Yoakum described Lew Webb, a first-rate wagon boss, as "a good level-headed fellow, never excited when things went wrong, and knew how to handle a herd at all times, day or night, in sunshine or rain." Many such individuals later became successful ranchers in their own right.

Because roundup crews tended to mirror their foremen in terms of personality, attentive leaders tended to elicit the best performance from their men, while careless and indifferent types fared poorly. Likewise, "top screws" who were overly critical, too severe or hot tempered risked losing those proud, often touchy hands, "too independent to take a 'cussin'.'" One former cowboy praised Handy P. Cole, wagon boss, and later superintendent of a major Texas outfit, not only for his smooth and consistent way of directing cow work, but also for a polite manner of giving orders that made his men feel that they were doing him a favor by complying.

Routine cowboy complaints about the long hours and hard work, however, usually went unheeded by even the most lenient foremen. In fact, many bosses took pride in having their wrangler gather the *remuda* for the day's work "before he could distinguish a horse from a tree stump" and in getting their crews in the saddle before sunup. Cowhands new to such outfits were sometimes advised to trade their bedrolls for lanterns because they were not going to sleep anyway.

Most ranchers worked their hands seven days a week, without showing much regard for the Sabbath. In the spring of 1888, however, the mammoth XIT spread made news in ranch country when management instituted a six-day work week.

A few miserly managers fed their men only twice daily during roundups, skipping breakfast or, more commonly, lunch. As late as the turn of the century, ranchers in the Southwest still fed their men on as little as one dollar per week per man.

A wagon boss usually assigned the mounts for his crew, six to twelve animals per man on average, depending upon the difficulty of the terrain and work. Many allowed top hands the privilege of picking their own strings on the basis of seniority with the outfit. Roundup hands usually changed mounts at least once or twice during the workday, and at times even more often. Horses ridden for a half a day in grueling country might be rested for two or three days before being called upon again. Cowboys also reserved some of their string for special tasks like roping, cutting and night work.

Large *remudas*, some consisting of several hundred horses, while scarce before the Civil War, became commonplace on late-nineteenth-century ranches. Even after fencing circumscribed the range, cow

The Allie Streeter Ranch sits nestled in a bend of Willow Creek near Nanton, Alberta.

work still required plenty of sound horseflesh, especially on substantial spreads with individual pastures covering tens of thousands of acres. Long distances, rough ground and wily cattle called for surefooted steeds with strength, stamina and intelligence.

Horses bred on the northern plains and in the Pacific Northwest tended to be larger than their compact Texas counterparts, the descendants of Spanish colonial imports. According to a correspondent for a Kansas newspaper writing in 1885, Montana hands rode

great big tallowy horses as sleek as livery horses, and very few of them but what are gentle as a dog. . . . Boys who have worked on both ranges say that while the average Texas cow pony cannot compare with his Montana brother as to looks, yet when it comes to doing hard work and a heap of it, he is far superior to the latter. He is quicker and harder, and better adapted to just such work.

Hay is left on the fields to dry on the TE Ranch in Cody, Wyoming.

Except for an occasional biscuit from the chuck box, few saddle horses consumed anything but grass. Some mounts would not even touch grain and had to be encouraged to eat it.

Put to hard use, horses suffered frequent injuries, with pulled tendons and broken legs being among the most common. Despite their natural agility, the mounts of southwestern "brush poppers" also endured nasty lacerations and imbedded cactus and mesquite thorns that led to serious infection if left unattended. During the winter months, ranchers allowed most of their *remudas* to recuperate from the roundup season, keeping only enough animals on hand to mount their camp men.

According to a former horse wrangler, the W outfit in Texas replaced about 75 animals in its 200-horse *remuda* annually because of injuries or old age. Some ranches bred their own replacement stock; others purchased fresh mounts each year at a cost of $30 to $35 in the 1890s. Those outfits that did not buy gentle animals employed professional bronc busters as needed to break the new acquisitions to saddle.

Horse breakers normally received the wages of a top hand, augmented by an additional fee, typically $2.50 to $5.00 for every horse tamed. Such incentives often encouraged busters to employ severe bits, stinging quirts and raking spurs to accomplish the task as quickly as possible. As few as three saddlings were considered sufficient to gentle a bronc to the point that it could be assigned to a cowboy's regular string for further training.

Although saddle horses were generally broken as two-year-olds, they did not mature into experienced all-round performers before the age of five or six. Some never made the grade, and almost every change of mounts witnessed some high-strung, bucking animals. "I rode 'Chicken' three years and didn't even tame him, much less gentle him," cowboy Brook Campbell remembered. "It was a fight every time I got on him and I had to ride him down every morning before he was worth a darn."

Only a few riders toughed out a career in the dangerous and physically demanding profession of bronc twister. One of the exceptions, Claud Jeffers of the Matador Ranch, broke as many as 3,500 horses during a thirty-year career. "Riding a bucking horse," quipped one practitioner, "is like having boils—you never get thoroughly used to it." Moreover, the job produced nose bleeds, ruptures, broken bones, bruised kidneys and disabling spinal injuries. "My main job around camps was to break wild horses," recalled one crippled bronc twister, "and I feel sure that is why I am in this invalid's chair today, even though many have done the same thing and are still going. I rode one old outlaw horse once and instead of hearing the usual sound of my neck a-poppin', it was my back and I'm sure some part of my spine was injured in a way that doctors have not been able to aid. . . ."

Cowboys used to horseback tasks, no matter how dangerous, rebelled at the thought of building fence, climbing windmills, scraping reservoirs, mowing hay and other forms of ground work required by the new ranching order. "As for milking," wrote one with indignation, "a cowboy would almost rather walk two miles and die of thirst." The rapidly shrinking domain of the cattleman, however, forced top hands who considered such tasks beneath their dignity to look for jobs among the relatively few "straight riding outfits" that had retreated to remote, wild, plow-resistant regions.

The harsh environmental lessons of the mid-1880s led ranchers to become increasingly interested in stock farming, range conservation and the development of water resources. These fledgling efforts represented individual rather than universal approaches, and varied widely in result. Small-scale ranchers with limited range and water usually embraced such techniques before their larger, better-endowed neighbors.

Most cattlemen drilled wells and erected windmills to tap underground aquifers, and created dams and earthen reservoirs to trap rain in enclosed pastures without benefit of natural creeks or springs. Range riders often accomplished and maintained these improvements during slack periods. Until the appearance of self-oiling windmills during the early twentieth century, cowboys bearing hip flasks full of lubricant could be observed climbing windmill towers weekly to grease the gears by hand. On a few large ranches professional windmillers regularly serviced the giant wheels.

Fencing and windmills allowed enlightened ranchers to rotate their stock from pasture to pasture to rest overgrazed range. Although a few resourceful cattle raisers would also launch fledgling reseeding projects, widespread scientific range management lay well in the future.

The decade of the 1880s and beyond also saw a rapid increase in the number of ranches investing in agricultural machinery and engaging in experimental farming. Such innovations not only augmented the food supply of their employees and herds, but also demonstrated the agricultural potential of their grassland. In 1887, for example, a two-acre garden on the Buffalo Springs division of the XIT Ranch yielded an astonishing array of cabbages, cucumbers, beets, onions, melons, squash, carrots, cauliflowers, radishes, lettuce, tomatoes, parsnips, beans and peas. Farm production on most ranches, however, meant fodder crops like hay, sorghum, millet, oats and kafir corn, which were fed to herds as a grazing supplement during droughts and difficult winters. Although hayracks eventually became as common as corrals and windmills on many ranges, the capital outlay required to sustain farm production, however beneficial, discouraged some ranchers.

The example of the Spur Ranch is perhaps illustrative of the diversified nature of work on the largest, best-financed and most innovative ranches by the 1890s. Employees of this West Texas spread performed seventeen different kinds of labor in 1891. Only about half worked with cattle and horses, and fewer than 22 percent in roundup and branding duties. Sixteen percent engaged in trail driving, 12 percent in fence and range riding, and 2 percent in horse wrangling. About a third of all hands worked on the ranch's feed and experimental farms. Tasks like cooking, fencing, tanking, blacksmithing, hauling and dairying occupied most of the rest.

Transient workers, employed for a short time, comprised between one-half and two-thirds of Spur Ranch employees during the course of any given year. The ranch employed more than 900 different hands between 1883 and 1909, an average of 33 per year. Of these individuals, 64 percent worked for only a single season, and another 20 percent for two seasons. Just 5 percent lasted as many as five years.

Only a small minority of cowboys spent their entire careers with the same ranch, or even in the same locale. Hispanic and African American hands who labored for *patróns* in the Southwest exhibited perhaps the greatest loyalty and longevity. Cowboys on the plains tended to drift from job to job, always anxious to see what lay beyond the horizon. The same held true for the mercurial trail-driver population. George Saunders, a well-informed former drover, estimated that only about one-third of his comrades on the northern trails ever repeated the experience. Fewer still lasted as many as five seasons, although William B. Slaughter, one of the anomalies, accompanied longhorn herds northward more than twenty times.

Maturity, misfortune and matrimony ended most cowboy careers before the age of forty. Although cowboy life offered ample adventure, the meager monetary rewards presented little incentive for many men of ability and drive. A pair of cowboys with loftier aspirations once sent seventy-five cents to a newspaper advertiser who promised to reveal the secret to making nearly a cowboy's monthly wage in a single day. One of the gullible punchers recalled receiving a cordial reply from the con artist suggesting that they "pick out one or two leading newspapers and advertise for suckers like I do."

Most punchers eventually traded life in the saddle for the economic and social responsibilities of marriage and family. "On my way home," said drover F.M. Polk, recalling his last trip up the trail, "I reviewed my past life as a cowboy from every angle and came to the conclusion that about all I had gained was experience, and that I could not turn into cash, so I decided I had enough of it, and made up my mind to go home, get married and settle down to farming."

Although some individuals remained on the range as managers, wagon cooks and freighters, many pursued livestock-related trades in towns, hanging out their shingles as butchers, commission merchants and livery-stable operators. A few, no doubt drawing on past experience, took up bartending. African American bronc buster "Bones" Hooks traded his Stetson for the cap of a train porter on the Santa Fe line. On at least one occasion, however, the lure of an outlaw bronc coaxed Hooks back into the saddle for a brief return to his former glory while his train and its passengers waited patiently at the station.

Hooks eventually became a distinguished citizen of Amarillo, Texas, where he helped establish the first black church and school. Indeed, many cowboys became substantial citizens of communities throughout the West. Their ranks produced bankers, churchmen, educators, mayors, judges, legislators and even governors. Although seldom a path to prosperity, cowboy life did not seem to impair future financial prospects either. Some 66 percent of a sample of fifty old-time cowboys interviewed in 1951, for example, described themselves as at least moderately prosperous.

Railroad-track layers signaled the transformation of ranch country from a fluid frontier backwater to a more connected and rooted society. The coming of the iron horse unleashed a host of land-hungry farmers who swarmed the Great Plains like the grasshoppers that sometimes devoured their crops. For a while some ranchers and their cowboys resisted the flood tide of "nesters" through propaganda and harassment, though rarely with violence.

Many cattle raisers encouraged their hands to file homestead claims on desirable acreage in order to preempt other settlers from buying it. Such tactics never proved effective for long, however, and the barriers, real and imagined, that once separated farmers and ranchers soon began to crumble. Indeed, the arrival of the "hoe men" enabled many hard-pressed cattlemen to scale back their operations or sell out completely, with the subsequent loss of riding jobs.

Cowboys, however, usually welcomed the new arrivals, who brought with them schools and churches and other trappings of civilization. Farm wives took in the ranch hands' laundry, sold them wild-fruit jelly and exchanged reading matter and news from the outside world. Of even more importance, cowpunchers also began to court their daughters.

The advent of the farmer's frontier introduced an unprecedented number of women into what had been a primarily masculine society under the tenure of cattlemen. R.L. Anderson recalled that, for two of the three years he spent punching cows in the Texas Panhandle during the early 1880s, he "never saw a woman's face." Bored cowboys on one ranch passed the time one winter answering "lonely heart" advertisements. "Some waddy that was good at writing love stuff would fix up the letters and they received some heart-breaking replies," recalled one of the correspondents.

By 1883, however, the *Texas Live Stock Journal* was reporting more promising female inroads among the cowboy population: "As the frontier of Texas has been gradually forced further and further west, the old time tramping ground of these knights of the lasso have, per force, been more thrown in control with the fair sex than in former years, and the effect has been to soften down their rugged natures, and to smooth the ragged edges of character otherwise admirable."

Even after the close of the open range, however, the nature of cow work—months of nomadic isolation—left buckaroos little time for steady courting, except during winter layoffs, infrequent visits to town and occasional dances held at ranches on special occasions or holidays like Christmas and the Fourth of July. Cowboys were known to ride sixty miles on horseback to attend even the most modest of these long-anticipated affairs, some of which lasted several days. The host always furnished plenty of food and drink, and each participant usually chipped in a dollar or two to pay the musicians, many of whom were cowboys themselves.

Despite the obstacles to long-term courting relationships, one Montana cowhand observed that "it was very seldom that a school marm taught the second term without annexing some cowboy for a husband, and as a rule they had the entire bunch to pick from." For cowboy grooms, marriage almost invariably signaled the end of life on the range. Very few nineteenth-century ranches would hire married hands, much less provide the amenities of house and home. In time, however, the world of automobiles, paved roads, horse trailers and telephones would help change such attitudes—but at the cost of other time-honored cowboy traditions.

THE
LEGACY

Built in 1876, the Barbara Watkins Reynolds house is one of many stone ranch houses still standing on the Lambshead Ranch in West Texas.

TOP LEFT: The JA Ranch in Texas is still owned and occupied by descendants of John Adair, one of the historic ranch's founding partners. Despite ranching 200,000 acres, the JA Ranch is one-fifth of its original size.

LEFT: The old JA cookhouse is still fixing meals.

LEFT: The cookhouse of the Gang Ranch in British Columbia.

LOWER LEFT: This log house on the TE Ranch near Cody, Wyoming, was once the home of Buffalo Bill.

UPPER RIGHT: The old Gardner ranch near High River, Alberta, sits in the foothills of the Rockies.

RIGHT: Cattle graze near the huge ranch house of the 6666 Ranch in Guthrie, Texas.

The Douglas Lake Cattle Company's general store.

The self-contained Douglas Lake Cattle Company has created its own small community in the Nicola Valley, British Columbia, with a general store, post office, school and housing for the ranch's employees.

An old stable near Ucross, Wyoming.

A cowboy clears the dirt from his horse's hooves outside his summer residence in British Columbia.

Buford, Colorado.

LEFT: The OH Ranch near High River, Alberta, is traditionally operated, requiring all vintage equipment to be well maintained.

A replica built from the original plans of an
1850s Las Vegas house. This ranch house, which
fuses rancho and Mississippi styles, is situated on
the Circle Diamond, in Picaho, New Mexico,
part of the Robert O. Anderson ranching
empire.

Living room of a ranch house on the Ladder
Ranch, near Truth or Consequences, New
Mexico.

The common room of
a resort ranch house in
Colorado.

Les Davis' family photographs portray a distinguished ranching dynasty at the CS Ranch, near Cimarron, New Mexico.

LEFT: A piano, an early symbol of civilized culture, sits in the parlor room of the ranch house on Pitchfork Ranch in Meeteetse, Wyoming.

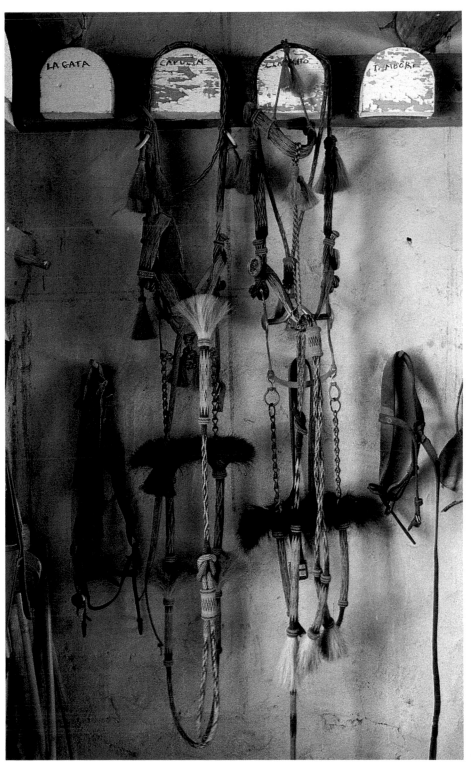

Hand-braided horsehair reins and bridles hanging at the
Sentinel Ranch, New Mexico.

LEFT: The austere dining room at the Sentinel Ranch in
San Patricio, New Mexico.

The dining room of the ranch house at the San Julian Rancho. The rancho was established in 1837 by Jose de la Guerra y Noriega, commander of the military presidio of Santa Barbara, and is still run by his family.

The furniture in the living room of the San Julian ranch house indicates the lively trading industry at the port of Santa Barbara, with antiques from China, Great Britain, South America, the Philippines and New England.

Dibblee Poett, heir to the de la Guerra estate, greets visitors to the San Julian Rancho.

The Forked Lightning Ranch has been modernized with bright paint to give it a contemporary Tex Mex feel, Pecos, New Mexico.

TOP: The fence posts of Forked Lightning sport the ranch's brand.

ABOVE: A waved wall recalls the early Spanish missions that raised cattle as far back as the seventeenth century.

RIGHT: Sage plants grow wild against the concrete walls of the ranch.

A corral near Patagonia, New Mexico.

New swinging gates lean against a log cabin wall,
Douglas Lake Cattle Company, British
Columbia.

ABOVE: A cowboy's Christmas wreath of sage, barbed wire and boot hangs from the front gate of the Mariposa Ranch near Cody, Wyoming.

LEFT: Although at first shunned owing to high prices and the fear of cattle injury, barbed wire became a necessity amongst ranchers as they cordoned off their grazing fields, changing cattle ranching from a free ranging enterprise to one of animal husbandry.

RIGHT: Baling wire lies in a discarded heap.

Pickups are as much a part of contemporary ranch
life as chuck wagons were over a century ago.

The productive lives of pickups are lengthened with spare parts salvaged from derelict vehicles.

The symbols of ranch life grace the sign boards,
water tanks and walls of ranch country.

Buford, Colorado.

A derelict ranch house near Mora, New Mexico.

Sculptural piles of used horseshoes at the Eaton dude ranch, Wolf, Wyoming.

A root cellar dug into a hillside for food storage before the days of refrigeration, Montana.

A long, low sheep shed near Choteau,
Montana.

Riding tackle hanging in the stable of the Perry Minor Ranch near Bindloss, Alberta.

A sod-roofed stable on the Perry Minor Ranch.

A homemade cow for junior cowboys to practice roping.

A ramshackle cookhouse made of logs and
aluminum siding sits on an isolated cow camp
far from the center of the Padlock Ranch in
Montana.

In contrast to its exterior, the cookhouse has a
comforting, homey feel, with only the propane
lamp and stove giving away the current era.

The traditional cookhouse dining room on the
Pitchfork Ranch, Texas.

The basic, yet efficient, kitchen on the
Pitchfork Ranch in West Texas.

ABOVE: The ranch house at Sentinel Ranch in New Mexico is based on the traditional Spanish design, with red tile roofs and buildings facing inwards to create a courtyard.

LEFT: A self-insulating, basic dugout made out of stone and adobe on the Sentinel Ranch, New Mexico.

ABOVE: A traditional mix of Mexican artifacts—Christian curios and desert finds—is displayed above a grain storage chest at the Sentinel ranch house in New Mexico.

RIGHT: A demon's face, or *debujo*, has been carved into a table top at the Sentinel Ranch.

ABOVE: Built in 1863, this grand two-story house of the Salman Ranch is nestled in the Sangre de Cristo mountains near Mora, New Mexico.

LEFT: The ranch house at the Doolittle Ranch in Watrous, New Mexico, was built by the town's namesake.

The original wing, on the left, of the ranch
house at the San Julian Rancho was built in
1805 and served as basic shelter for priests and
soldiers traveling from Santa Barbara.

ABOVE AND LEFT: The tack room at the CS Ranch near Cimarron, New Mexico.

The long cookhouse and bunkhouse porch on the OW Ranch, Decker, Montana.

A tombstone at Galisteo, New Mexico.

THE LEGACY

From the moment barbed wire first cast its thorny shadow on the plains, cowboys appeared to be headed for extinction. The economic and environmental calamities that befell the range-cattle industry during the 1880s reinforced this notion and, by the turn of the century, such distinguished mourners as Theodore Roosevelt, Owen Wister and Frederic Remington were lamenting the passing of the hired man on horseback and evoking his heroic spirit in literature and art. "He rides in his historic yesterday," Owen Wister wrote in the preface to his influential novel *The Virginian*. "You will no more see him gallop out of the unchanging silence than you will see Columbus on the unchanging sea come sailing from Palos in his caravels."

Cowboys had not disappeared, of course, but had merely adapted to new conditions. Still, these pastoral throwbacks seemed strangely out of place in the increasingly mechanical and urban world of the twentieth century. To successive generations of Americans, therefore, cowpunchers always seemed to be doomed to oblivion. Yet premature magazine and newspaper obituaries, bearing such titles as "The Passing of the Cowboy" (1898), "Passing of the Texas Cowboy and the Big Ranches" (1905), "The Vanishing Cowboy" (1909), "The Vanished Cowboy" (1920), "The Cowboy That Was" (1922) and "The Last Figure to Vanish" (1922), only confirmed the cowboy's resilience.

By this time, mellow memories of shared experience had prompted ex-cowboys in many regions to form fraternal associations that furnished members and their families an opportunity not only to socialize, but also to commemorate their accomplishments. One such group, the ExOpen Range Cowpunchers' Association, whose membership was limited to those who punched cattle in West Texas prior to 1880, was organized in 1905. Another, the Northwest Texas Cowboy Reunion, dated its origins to June 5, 1910.

In 1915, San Antonio cattle-commission merchant George

Saunders, a former cowboy and drover, founded the largest and most successful of these groups, the Old Time Trail Drivers' Association. Within five years the organization boasted more than 1,000 members. With the membership's help in the 1920s, Saunders published *The Trail Drivers of Texas*, a multivolume work containing the reminiscences and profiles of more than 300 individual drovers. In 1932, the organization successfully marked the site of historic Doan's Crossing on the Red River, part of the Great Western Cattle Trail to Kansas. More grandiose plans for a monumental sculpture honoring cattle drovers in San Antonio failed during the Great Depression for a lack of funds.

Despite the inroads of fences and farmers, more than 7 million cattle still roamed the western plains in 1900. Texas led all states in beef production, with more than 4 million head, and kept more than half of its nearly 270,000 square miles grass-side up. Giant ranches, although their numbers had thinned appreciably during the previous decade and a half, still dotted the Lone Star landscape. Sixty-two western Texas counties alone boasted some thirteen ranches, with herds ranging from 30,000 to 100,000 head, and more than seventy individual spreads pasturing 3,000 bovines each.

Large operators employed the greatest number of hands in their most traditional roles, although, as a writer for one national journal observed in 1901, cattle ranching required "more territory and fewer human workers than any other industry." The advent of automobiles during the first decade of the twentieth century would decrease that labor requirement even further.

Conservative ranchers eyed motor vehicles with suspicion at first. "The average cowman," wrote a correspondent for the *Denver Post*, "will stick to the old method of doing things, with the tenacity of a bulldog and he is the last to jump at new-fangled ideas, including automobiles and other kinds of machinery." Like other Americans, however, cattle raisers soon discovered the time- and labor-saving advantages of the horseless carriage.

In 1909, for example, two West Texas ranches ordered ten automobiles between them after conducting tests over a six-month period to determine the types best adapted for roundup use. A prominent cattleman, meanwhile, pronounced cars to be less disturbing to cow herds than were men on horseback. At least one imaginative trail boss tested that theory when, mounted in a Ford roadster, he led a drive of 1,100 head of wild horses, followed by five mounted drovers, from San Angelo, Texas, to the Mexican border.

By 1916, cowboys on the 187,000-acre San Cristobel Ranch at Lamy, New Mexico, employed automobiles, and even motorcycles, to ride fence, check windmills and search for strays during roundups. Although the ranch still maintained a traditional *remuda* for horseback work, the San Cristobel manager estimated that motorized transportation allowed his seven cowboys to do the work thirty-five or forty hands would have managed under the old system. Hauling cowboys from task to task by car not only reduced the size of *remudas*, but also helped prolong the working life of now better-bred and -fed saddle horses by three to five years.

When appealing to the ranch market, shrewd automobile advertisers often likened their products to fine horses. One Lincoln Motor Company ad in a prominent ranching publication called its new phaeton model "a car for wide, open spaces— for our own cattle country. All the restless energy and fire of a mustang cowpony is found in the Lincoln. Quick to turn and dash away, it will carry you at amazing speed over cow trails or boulevards."

After the First World War, trucks began to replace freight wagons as a means of conveying provisions and gear over the long distances between towns and ranches, and between ranch headquarters and outlying camps. Such conveyances made daily trips possible where previously weekly or monthly journeys had to suffice, and they allowed cattlemen to make do with fewer camps and supply them more quickly. As late as 1921, however, fewer than 4 percent of farms and ranches in the seventeen western states owned trucks, compared with more than 44 percent that had automobiles. And as late as 1930, a few diehard outfits still relied totally upon wagons to haul their goods.

Within a few years, ranches from Montana to Texas also began replacing animal-powered chuck wagons with motorized types, most by simply attaching a conventional wooden chuck box to a light truck or pickup. By 1932, only two large ranches in the vast Big Bend country of Texas still fed their hands from team-drawn chuck

155

wagons. The rest used trucks.

Sturdier and more powerful automobiles and pickups, fitted with low-pressure balloon tires, traveled rapidly over improving ranch-road systems with ever greater ease. Oil exploration accelerated the road-building process in many corners of ranch country, as did the development of cattle guards, which alleviated the necessity for opening and shutting gates.

As paved farm-to-market highways also proliferated, trucking began competing with railroads in the delivery of cattle to market. This development further curtailed the necessity to drive livestock long distances. Between 1924 and 1931, the amount of livestock trucked to major markets quadrupled, to more than 21 million head, and, within five years, trucks were transporting about half of western livestock to market, a proportion that continued to rise.

From a social perspective, automobiles relieved the historic isolation of pastoral life and offered ranch folk, like other Americans, greater freedom to explore what lay beyond the horizon. Without cars, a 1924 advertisement for the Chevrolet Motor Company warned, "they are prisoners on a limited range—like hobbled horses in a pasture." According to a report on Texas cow country published five years later, "nearly every ranch hand now owns some kind of car or has a friend who can be depended upon for a 'lift.'" Access to an automobile, the article continued, proved indispensable to a cowboy, whose social life was "largely governed by his distance from the home of his fair charmer."

Automobiles enabled cowboys to drift more widely in search of work, thereby saving on the cost of caring for a mount between jobs, and providing a place to stow saddle gear en route. Reliable cars, some coupled to homemade horse trailers, also made it possible for a few talented hands to compete in the now flourishing sport of rodeo. Nevertheless, a few footloose loners still roamed about on horseback into the 1930s, leading antiquated pack animals and preferring day work to steady employment.

Besides their legitimate uses, motor vehicles also afforded rustlers unprecedented mobility. It became a simple matter to cut a fence and hustle a few head of cattle into a trailer or truck by means of a chute gate or a crane and swing harness. Paved roads, moreover, obscured the trail of the modern rustler, making apprehension and conviction more difficult and challenging for law-enforcement officials.

Motor vehicles and paved highways were but two links in the communications chain that connected ranches and cowboys with the outside world during the first quarter of the twentieth century. Telephones had had their initial impact on ranch life nearly two decades earlier, when a few innovative ranchers began stringing lines along barbed-wire fences to link their secluded line camps with headquarters. As early as 1884, a private line joined the Prairie Cattle Company field headquarters with Trinidad, Colorado. Lightning and damp fence posts, however, frequently grounded the current of the battery-powered, hand-cranked devices, curtailing service during periods of inclement weather. Regardless, telephone lines facilitated all types of business transactions, from ordering supplies to summoning help, to ascertaining weather, grass and market conditions. They also permitted greater interaction among the often socially isolated female population of ranch country. In 1919, the manager of the SMS outfit expressed his opinion that telephones had "done more for ranch women than any other factor."

At least a few primitive phonographs had also found their way onto the range in advance of horseless carriages, bringing both traditional tunes and the latest popular music to cow camps throughout the West. One former cowhand recalled the unsettling appearance of a ranch official from the East, his "talking machine" in tow. "When he arrived," the former puncher recalled, "the boys had all either gone to sleep or out on night guard . . . and [when] he turned it on out there under the midnight skies . . . all the punchers stampeded." In the early 1890s, fascinated and bewildered hands on the XIT Ranch lined up to pay a traveling photographer five cents each to listen to cylinder recordings, their sound emanating from rubber tubes hooked to a player. The strains of "The Bird on Nellie's Hat" and "The Arkansas Traveler," played nightly through the red horn of a range cook's new Victor talking machine, enlivened the mess tent of one northern plains outfit.

Thanks to sound recordings and battery-operated radios, a new generation of cowboys added modern steps like the Hesitation and the Fox Trot to their dance cards. Radios brought the ranch and

157

ABOVE: Now replaced by a hay baler, this stackloader is an imposing artifact on the Gang Ranch, British Columbia.

LEFT: Tack room with rustic hooks at the Cartwright Ranches, Alberta.

ABOVE: Fuel drums.

RIGHT: The chuck
wagon is rarely used for
practical reasons on
contemporary ranches.

range not only music, but also a wide variety of popular programming, livestock reports and sporting events.

During the early days of motion pictures, many out-of-work cowboys drifted to Hollywood, where they found employment as extras and stuntmen in silent westerns. Others performed in movies filmed on location in various parts of the West to take advantage of natural scenery and authentic characters. In 1916, famed rancher Charles Goodnight produced a loosely autobiographical movie of his own, titled *Old Texas*, which included scenes of real cowboys roping buffalo. The 1924 film version of Emerson Hough's *North of '36* featured a herd of 5,000 genuine longhorn cattle, part of the rapidly dwindling remnant of that once prolific breed. Unruly grass fires set for authenticity during a 1938 remake of the same film burned twenty square miles of Texas range before being brought under control.

Although often critical of motion-picture portrayals of their kind, many cowboys loved movies. They also idolized early silent stars like William S. Hart, who dressed authentically for his cowboy roles. By the late 1920s, however, more colorful western-movie costuming, in tandem with shrewd manufacturers and merchandisers, blurred regional differences in cowboy dress and produced a uniform standard embraced by a new generation of cowboys. "If life did not entirely imitate the movies," film historian Kevin Brownlow observed, "at least a fragment of fiction had splintered into fact."

Military service in the First World War also provided many cowboys with new perspectives on the world. When the United States declared war on Germany in 1917, cowpunchers joined their countrymen in volunteering, most, no doubt, hoping for cavalry duty. The SMS Ranch, for example, lost twenty-three employees, mostly cowboys, described by one company official as "the very cream of our best skilled men and all splendid specimens of physical manhood." Ranchers naturally tried to retain their top hands to train unskilled replacements. A few cattle raisers lost their entire cadre to the armed forces. Ray Morley, one of those unfortunates, endured the good-natured ribbing of his New Mexico neighbors, who referred to his Drag A crew as "Morley's kindergarten outfit."

The war-induced shortage of skilled cowboy labor persisted into

1919, as some units remained in Europe after hostilities ceased. While they waited, two Montana cowboys serving with U.S. occupation forces in Germany sought mounts with which to become the first cowpunchers to swim the 400-yard wide Rhine River on horseback.

A severe downturn in the cattle market accompanied the Armistice declaration of November 1918. Many cattlemen who had overexpanded while the war in Europe raged now could not meet their obligations amid deflated prices. Seventy-five percent of ranchers in some regions of the West went broke, much of their land being sold off to farmers. One West Texas realtor's automobile bore a sign of the times that read: "Cowboy dismount and let the farmer ride the plains."

In the difficult years that followed, conservative ranches survived thanks to good fortune and good management. The timely discovery of oil sustained some cattle operations, although higher-paying oil-field jobs lured many of their cowhands away from the range.

During the late 1920s, the cattle market had rebounded from its postwar doldrums only to plunge again with the onset of the Great Depression. Between 1929 and 1932, beef prices fell by more than 50 percent, signaling a new round of foreclosures. Grass disappeared even faster under a withering drought that lasted five parched years or more in some regions. The prolonged aridity severely reduced the cattle-carrying capacity of southern plains ranges.

During stressful winters, when grass usually was sparsest, cowboys fed silage or cottonseed cake to cattle "too thin to cast a shadow." Many herds in the Southwest subsisted on fiber-rich and water-retentive prickly pear, its thorns singed away by cowboys bearing army flamethrowers or special pear burners fueled by gasoline or kerosene. At roundup time, cowpunchers adapted the brass-tanked burners to heat their branding irons.

A few drought-stricken ranchers were able to truck or drive their herds to fresh pasture, sometimes several hundred miles away. Although increasingly rare after the spread of barbed wire, cattle drives were occasionally revived when the cost of truck and rail transport proved prohibitive.

Three riders and a chuck-wagon cook accompanied one such herd of 600 head on a forty-eight-day drive from Big Wells, Texas, to a new

ABOVE: Whimsical prints tacked to the wall of an abandoned bunkhouse near White Springs, Montana.

BELOW: Wagon wheels are a favorite decorative object in ranch country. Here at the OH Ranch, the design possibilities are pushed to the limit with a table top, lazy susan and chandelier all made from the spoked wheels.

OPPOSITE PAGE TOP: The carved cantle of G.R. Roberts' saddle.

OPPOSITE PAGE BOTTOM LEFT: A highly detailed, antique saddle handmade by the master craftsman G.R. Roberts of Helena, Montana.

OPPOSITE PAGE BOTTOM RIGHT: Bert Sheppard of the OH Ranch in Alberta reminisces about the evolution of ranch life from the open range to cattle farming.

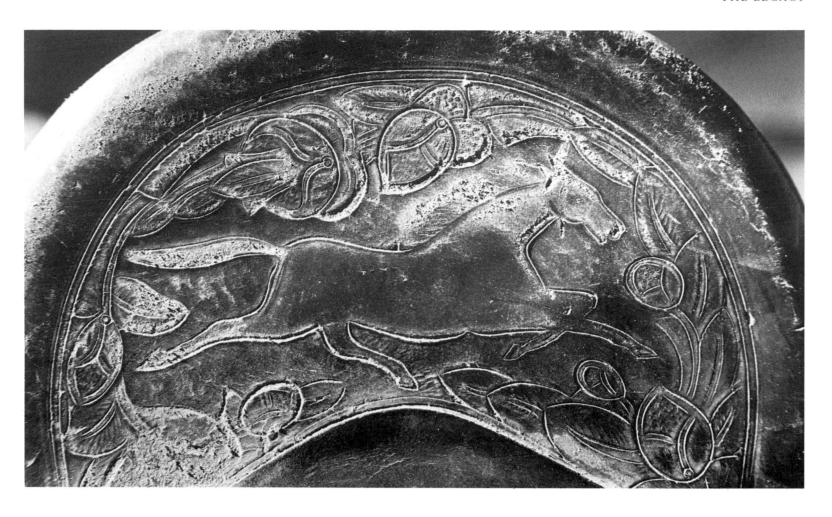

home range in Blanco County in November 1937. The modern-day drovers, who included Lucile Cowan, wife of trail boss J.H. Cowan, covered only four or five miles per day, often in the face of driving sleet and rain. Castroville residents with rowboats helped the beleaguered crew cross the Medina River, a difficult feat that lasted from midmorning until midnight. Many animals drowned in the process, and others later died of exposure. About 20 percent of the herd was abandoned along the route.

With the onset of the drought, ranchers began to reduce both their herds and their hands, retaining only a skeleton workforce. Cowboys who commanded $60 monthly in 1929 now accepted as little as $15, and some, simply grateful for jobs, worked for only food and shelter. Hard times demanded other concessions from frugal cowhands already used to patching their clothing and gear to make them last. They now rationed their tobacco, hoarded precious liquor for special occasions and hunted to supplement scanty ranch provisions.

Federal intervention reduced livestock numbers and precipitated a rise in cattle prices beginning in 1934. Although drought continued to plague some areas until 1938, the Depression gradually ebbed, improving ranchers' bottom lines and returning monthly earnings for top hands to as much as $60 before the end of the decade. Day laborers drew $2, $3 if they supplied their own horses. By this time, however, competition from New Deal work programs made it difficult even for ranchers paying top wages to retain adequate range help.

Although they comprised fewer than 3 percent of all cattle outfits, the largest western ranches remained bastions of cowboy tradition. In the early 1930s, *vaqueros* on the million-and-a-quarter-acre King Ranch still worked 80,000 head of stock cattle. A few sizable operations kept roundup crews occupied from April until Christmas without a break. The 800-section Matador Ranch maintained three wagons in the field the year round and branded more than 15,000 calves annually. Cowboys on the Four Sixes and Triangle ranches spent each July and August, between the spring and fall roundups, creating and repairing water systems, harvesting feed crops and filling trench silos. They occupied the period from the close of the roundup in mid-December until the following spring with the breaking and training of horses for their own *remudas* and for sale to other ranches.

Besides traditional range chores, cowboys on ranches lying below the national quarantine line dipped their herds, at fourteen- to twenty-one-day intervals, in concrete vats filled with chemicals designed to kill ticks bearing splenetic fever. The national dipping plan adopted in 1905 became widespread by 1914 and continued until the last vestiges of the disease were eradicated in Texas in the late 1940s. An efficient dipping crew could process 2,000 steers in about three hours.

Cowboys also manned the front line in the scientific assault on a host of other livestock ailments ranging from blackleg to hoof-and-mouth disease, to screw worms. This last scourge had cost southwestern cattlemen an estimated $4 million a year by the mid-1920s. Screw-worm flies appeared annually in early spring, laying their eggs in exposed tissue. A fear of infection caused some ranchers to delay branding, castrating and dehorning until late fall, by which time the insect had usually disappeared. Until the 1960s, when science rid the range of this destructive pest, vigilant cowboys, their roping skills again in demand, prowled pastures in search of infected animals in need of treatment.

Screw worms flourished in the thorn-infested regions of the Southwest, where mesquite obscured wild cattle from the prying eyes of the fearless "brush poppers" sent to gather them. Pasture work in brush country generally required two or three times more riders than in open terrain. Following packs of baying hounds, seasoned horsemen clad in duck jackets and heavy leather leggings pursued the feral bovines, which, when cornered or roped, often attacked their pursuers, occasionally killing horses and riders. "None of these Mexicans here get any kick out of a rodeo," one South Texas rancher observed, "for they have them every day while catching these cattle."

The western cattle industry had scarcely begun to recover from the depths of the Depression when the manpower demands of the Second World War produced a general shortage of skilled cowboy labor. By early 1943, Texas ranchers on average had lost about a third of their manpower and had reduced their operations by about 25 percent. The problem worsened as the war dragged on, though improvised crews of boys, women and imported Mexican labor willing to work for half wages tried to take up the slack.

The inexperience of these greenhorns, many of whom could not bridle a horse, much less conduct an efficient roundup, often exasperated the few experienced overseers left in charge. Tom Blasingame, a twenty-five-year veteran of the range at the time, ran the JA Ranch roundup wagon during the war. "It'd drive a man crazy, working with them kind of fellars," Blasingame recalled years later. "They didn't do nothing right. Didn't take care of their horses. They'd get lost on drives, and you'd have to go back and hunt them. I quit that as soon as I could."

With husbands and sons off to war, women played greater roles in range work than before, often while maintaining their traditional household responsibilities. One ranch wife from the Big Bend region of Texas broke her hand while branding, but in true cowboy style refused to leave the work until the last hide sizzled. After suffering a painful rope burn on another occasion, she remembered cursing "for all I could think of and almost shocked my husband out of the saddle."

As the war continued, competition from high-paying factory jobs threatened to tap the shallow pool of agricultural labor even more than the draft. A modest rise in cowboy pay after the Depression paled in comparison with the 157 percent increase in the average factory wage between 1939 and 1942. Ranchers competed as much as price controls and their own financial means and conservative natures would allow. Ranch hands drawing $60 a month and buying their own food in 1942 demanded up to $150 plus rations in 1944. Some ranches even gave Christmas bonuses in order to help retain hands. Beset by labor woes, rancher J. Evetts Haley wrote to a friend in February 1944:

> For a year and more I have made a practice of hiring every single man who came along who said he wanted to work. Sometimes they last a week. The young bucks wont stay in the country past Saturday afternoon, and if they will, they wont work. They are not worth killing. The army is what they need, and in all my effort, I haven't found one up here yet that had the simple determination and interest in a job

Driving cattle across the highway on the Irvine Ranch in California.

to work. Yet I walked into a pool hall in the village of Spearman two weeks ago, and counted over 30 men and boys there, playing or sweating the games at mid-afternoon, and it wasn't Saturday, either.

The largest ranches suffered the most from such inexperience. "The expected shortage of men has worried me a great deal," Pitchfork Ranch manager Rudolph Swenson wrote to a fellow cattleman, "and I have given a lot of thought to methods by which we could do our work with a smaller crew." Motor vehicles might have compensated more for scarce labor had not gasoline rationing and parts shortages made travel and supply difficult, particularly for remote ranches, some of which lay fifty miles or more from the nearest town. Bosses like Swenson did the best they could, scaling down pastures with more cross-fencing and depending more heavily upon labor-saving machinery for livestock work. Such devices as branding tables and dehorning chutes required about 50 percent less crew and experience to brand, castrate, dehorn and doctor stock than did traditional methods that depended upon the skillful execution of ropers and flankers. Beyond their labor-saving qualities, such tools were generally considered a more sanitary way to work cattle than the traditional methods of roping and dragging calves to the branding fire. By the 1940s, manufacturers had produced several different types of branding and dehorning tables and chutes, some with sling and roller attachments to facilitate veterinary procedures and hoof trimming. In early 1942, a North Texas rancher reported that a crew of five inexperienced men chute-branded fifty-eight calves in two and one-half hours using a device of his own invention. He thought an experienced team of seven or eight men could easily handle fifty to seventy-five calves an hour—"never lay a calf down, never bruise a calf and certainly never bruise a man, and even the horse will stand out tied to the fence all the time that you are doing the work."

The employment trends set in motion by the Second World War persisted in the immediate postwar era. By 1945 more than 99 percent of the labor force was employed. The modest rise in cowboy wages resulting from prosperous economic conditions, however, could not offset the effects of high urban employment, the GI bill and the broadened worldview of returning veterans. Even the centuries-old *patrón* system in the Southwest broke down in the face of rapid urbanization and the precipitous decline of the rural population in the wake of war.

Although ranches could not expect to retain married hands for long without suitable housing, as late as the 1930s a few traditionalists still believed matrimony to be incompatible with the demands of ranch work. "This was a little hard on Cupid," one ranch executive admitted, "but it was best for the cows." Other managers, however, had long argued that wedded cowboys were more stable and dependable than their single counterparts. Regardless, most large ranches were ill prepared to accommodate the influx of married personnel during the Second World War. One prominent West Texas outfit housed overflow couples in converted railroad boxcars until the ranch could erect more suitable quarters. Even as late as the 1950s, kerosene lamps still supplied the light, outhouses the sanitary facilities, and cool creek water and beneficent shade trees the refrigeration for cow camps beyond the reach of electric lines and indoor plumbing.

Single cowboys, who continued to live outdoors or in tents for months on end, generally fared even worse. Spartan bunkhouses at most ranch headquarters offered little privacy and few amenities. Until the late 1940s, only a few cattle raisers could afford to emulate the oil-wealthy Waggoner Ranch, which, a decade earlier, had provided its unmarried men with a modern stone dormitory complete with showers, natural gas, electric lights and a refrigerator.

Facing a persistent dearth of hands from the 1940s onward, ranches relied more heavily than ever on motorized cowboys equipped with pickups and stock trailers. The conveying of horses to and from the range enabled some ranchers to trim their *remudas* by between 40 and 50 percent. The postwar era also witnessed airplane- and helicopter-assisted roundups, although the practice may have begun as early as 1916, when a New Mexico rancher negotiated the purchase of an aircraft to help him keep track of his herds. Flying machines proved particularly valuable in locating and flushing fugitive livestock from rough terrain and dense vegetation. Before the appearance of two-way radios, pilots communicated to riders below by means of loudspeakers.

By 1960, old-fashioned chuck wagons and the way of life that attended them had all but disappeared. Although in later years sentimental ex-cowboys often recalled the chuck-wagon era with fondness, most welcomed the improved living conditions that postwar prosperity made possible. "You've never seen such a footrace as you did at the end of the day," said one employee recalling the moment when pickups first began to carry hands to the Waggoner Ranch bunkhouse for the night.

With the approach of a new century, old questions about the continued viability of cowboy life again obtrude. Pessimists wonder if professional pride and Americans' enduring appetite for beef will be enough to sustain the breed in the next century. The certain impact of science and technology and the fickle fortunes of the economy and the environment render hasty judgments risky. For now at least, cowboys still have a role to play in the world of grass and cattle.

Cattle drive, Padlock
Ranch, Montana.

Julia-Lyn Davis relaxes at the CS Ranch.

Linda Davis hauling hay on the CS Ranch,
Cimarron, New Mexico.

RIGHT: Bobby Gibbs of the Powder River
region, Wyoming, was forced out of the sheep
business by predators and government interfer-
ence.

In a few raucous minutes a calf is roped, thrown
and held down as a traditional branding—including ear notching, vaccination and dehorning—is
undertaken at the Douglas Lake Cattle Company,
British Columbia.

Heating the branding irons.

Mike Ferguson considers the cowboy life an
aging, yet healthy, experience.

Veterinary students get hands-on experience at the Douglas Lake Cattle Company in British Columbia.

ABOVE: Antiseptic aerosol is held at the ready.

RIGHT: A cowgirl performs a quick castration, determining this calf's destiny as beef.

Padlock Ranch,
Wyoming.

Udo Schneider of Alberta holds a couple of Australian sheep dog puppies.

Rick Ortega of the
Ladder Ranch, New
Mexico.

Warren Zimmerman of Alberta.

OVERLEAF: Taking a break during a day of branding at the JA Ranch, Texas.

Cedar Nolan, foreman
of the F Cross Ranch,
Texas.

On the ranch, boots take a beating.

Frank Gattey and
his wife, Kelva (*left*),
run the Simmenthal
herd on the Cross
Bar Ranch, Consort,
Alberta.

187

Denim drying in the sun.

Hip waders for fishing—a slower paced activity for
the cowboy's free time.

Overleaf: Sitting back after a long day of branding at the Douglas Lake Cattle Company, British
Columbia.

A real cowboy starts young.

Watching the rodeo.

Veteran cowboy, Ken Smith—displaying horsehair bridles and guitar straps he plaited himself—has driven cattle from Canada to Mexico five times during his long career.

Detail of a braided
horsehair bridle.

Rita Hill and her daughter Janaloo graze eighty-seven cattle in the ghost town of Shakespeare, New Mexico. To augment their income, the Hills run a ballet school for girls from neighboring Lordsburg.

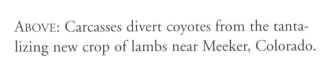
ABOVE: Carcasses divert coyotes from the tantalizing new crop of lambs near Meeker, Colorado.

RIGHT: Former cowboy Bill Sallee sells coyote pelts on the Ladder Ranch, New Mexico.

ABOVE: A coyote stands alert on the wildlife preserve of the McIntyre Ranch, Alberta.

LEFT: Bill Austin, the coyote hunter for Johnson County, Wyoming, lures the coyote within range.

Almost 60,000 Canada geese descend upon
the Bolak Ranch in Farmington, New Mexico,
each winter.

Wildlife from around the world are frozen in action
and mounted on display in this trophy room.

Snake hunter Jimmy Nolan on the F Cross
Ranch, Texas.

A cowboy at the Douglas Lake Cattle Company.

Miles of rope at King Ropes, Sheridan, Wyoming.

The saddle room at King Ropes.

ABOVE: Yearlings weather the storm.

LEFT: Every winter ranchers must expect to lose a few head of cattle due to unexpected storms, hungry predators and disease.

A newborn calf lies stunned in the thawing spring
snows, as its mother prods it into awareness.